THE PURPOSE OF
Christmas

THE PURPOSE OF
Christmas

RICK WARREN

HOWARD BOOKS
A Division of Simon & Schuster

NEW YORK ✦ LONDON ✦ TORONTO ✦ SYDNEY

Our purpose at Howard Books is to:
- *Increase faith* in the hearts of growing Christians
- *Inspire holiness* in the lives of believers
- *Instill hope* in the hearts of struggling people everywhere

Because He's coming again!

 Published by Howard Books, a division of Simon & Schuster, Inc.
HOWARD 1230 Avenue of the Americas, New York, NY 10020
BOOKS www.howardpublishing.com

The Purpose of Christmas © 2008 Rick Warren

Library of Congress Control Number: 200832575

ISBN-13: 978-1-4165-5900-9
ISBN-10: 1-4165-5900-0

10 9 8 7 6 5 4 3 2 1

HOWARD and colophon are registered trademarks of Simon & Schuster, Inc.

Manufactured in the United States of America

For information regarding special discounts for bulk purchases, please contact:
Simon & Schuster Special Sales at 1-800-456-6798 or business@simonandschuster.com.

Edited by Denny Boultinghouse
Cover design by John Lucas

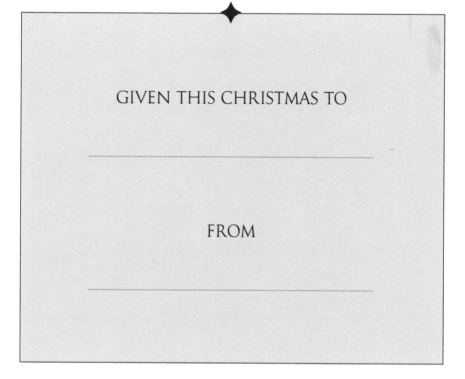

GIVEN THIS CHRISTMAS TO

....

FROM

....

Friends love through all kinds of weather,
and families stick together
in all kinds of trouble.

PROVERBS 17:17 *THE MESSAGE*

This book is dedicated
to those who will accept,
unwrap, and enjoy
God's Christmas gift for us.
Merry Christmas!

CONTENTS

THE PURPOSE OF

Christmas

To every thing there is a season,
and a time to every purpose
under the heaven.

ECCLESIASTES 3:1 KJV

WHY IS CHRISTMAS SUCH A BIG DEAL?

I t's the largest celebration around the world each year. Other holidays get a single day, but Christmas is emphasized for an entire month, one twelfth of every year. During the Christmas season, billions of people set aside their normal routines to decorate their homes, send out greeting cards, buy gifts, go to Christmas parties, attend church services, sing Christmas songs, watch Christmas TV specials, and travel long distances to be with their families. Christmas sights and sounds fill the air everywhere. There are stores, and even careers, that are exclusively dedicated to preparing for and celebrating this holiday. When Christmas comes, you can't miss it. It's everywhere.

If you stop to think about it, it is astounding that the simple, unassuming birth of a peasant boy born two thousand years ago in the Middle East has caused such commotion—his birthday even causes traffic jams today in places like New York City, Tokyo, and Rio de Janeiro.

You may have never realized that every time you check your calendar or refer to a date or write one down, you are using Jesus Christ as your reference point. Because of Jesus, history is divided into BC (*before Christ*) and AD (*anno Domini, in the year of the Lord*). Every other event in history and every event on your calendar today is dated by how many days and years it has been since Jesus Christ appeared on earth.

Even *your* birthday is dated by *his* birthday.

The night Jesus Christ was born in Bethlehem, a small group of poor shepherds was quietly tending their flocks of sheep in a nearby field. Looking up at the stars, nothing seemed any different from a thousand other nights. But what was about to happen would transform not only the shepherds' lives but billions of other lives as well. The world would never be the same. Suddenly a bright light lit up the sky, and an angel from God appeared above them and began speaking to them. It seemed unbelievable and scared them.

The Bible gives us the original Christmas story:

There were shepherds living out in the fields nearby, keeping watch over their flocks at night. An angel of the Lord appeared to them, and the glory of the Lord shone around them, and they were terrified. But the angel said to them, "Do not be afraid. I bring you good news of great joy that will be for all the people. Today in the town of David a Savior has been born to you; he is Christ the Lord. This will be

*a sign to you: You will find a baby wrapped in
cloths and lying in a manger."*

*Suddenly a great company of the heavenly
host appeared with the angel, praising God
and saying, "Glory to God in the highest, and
on earth peace to men on whom his favor
rests."*

LUKE 2:8–14 NIV

The angel said that Christmas would bring *"great
joy . . . for all the people."* Really? For many people, getting
ready for Christmas seems more of a hassle than a source
of happiness. It is a source of stress. They feel pressure,
not pleasure, when it comes to Christmas. It's a duty, not
a delight. They endure Christmas rather than enjoy it.

There are many possible reasons you might feel
uneasy or lonely or even depressed during the Christmas season. You may dread spending time with oddball
relatives. Maybe relationships are strained and uncom-

fortable in your family. Maybe you don't have anyone to be with this Christmas. Christmas may remind you of losses or hurts or how things have changed. You may have a religious background that doesn't include Christmas, or you may have no faith at all; watching others celebrate may make you feel uneasy. Maybe you're just exhausted and worn out from all that's happened in your life this past year. This Christmas, God cares deeply about how you feel, and so do I. It's why I have written this book.

Regardless of your background, religion, problems, or circumstances, Christmas really is the best news you could get. Beneath all the visible sights and sounds of Christmas are some simple yet profound truths that can transform your life for the better here on earth and for forever in eternity. Right now there's nothing more important for you to understand than the implications of Christmas for your life.

If you'll slow down for a few minutes, take the time

to read this brief book, and pause to consider the purpose of Christmas, you can receive and enjoy the best Christmas gift you'll ever be given. It is God's Christmas gift to you.

God's Christmas gift to you has three qualities that make it unique. First, it is the most expensive gift you'll ever receive. It's priceless. Jesus paid for it with his life. Second, it's the only gift you'll ever receive that will last *forever*. Finally, it is an extremely practical gift—one you'll use every day for the rest of your life. Interested?

It is no accident that you are reading this book. God planned your birth, and before you were even born, he knew this moment was coming. In fact, it may be that all your whole life up to this moment has been preparing you to receive God's Christmas gift to you.

On the first Christmas night, the angel announced three purposes for the birth of Jesus:

Christmas is a time for celebration!

Christmas is a time for salvation!

Christmas is a time for reconciliation!

A TIME FOR

Celebration

This is the day of the Lord's victory;

let us be happy, let us celebrate!

PSALM 118:24 TEV

Christmas is a party. Specifically, it's a *birthday party*—for Jesus—and birthdays are meant to be celebrated. It's why we say "*Merry* Christmas!"

Ironically, at most Christmas parties the person whose birthday we're supposed to be celebrating is completely ignored. He's never even mentioned. Although Jesus is the reason for the season, he's often overlooked or merely mentioned along with Rudolph, Frosty the Snowman, Santa Claus, the Grinch, elves, and a long list of celebrated fictional characters.

As I was writing this little book, I decided to take a survey of Christmas shoppers. I asked, "What are you celebrating this Christmas?" Most answers had nothing to do with Jesus:

- ❖ "I'm celebrating that I made it through another year."

- ❖ "I'm celebrating being home with my family."

- ❖ "I got a Christmas bonus."

- ❖ "My son is home from Iraq."

- ❖ "The candidate I voted for got elected."

- ❖ "I'm celebrating that I've finished all my shopping."

- ❖ "I'm not celebrating anything. I'm just trying to survive."

Preparing for Christmas can be a lot of work, especially for moms. With the pressure of buying gifts, sending greeting cards, decorating our homes, putting up lights, cooking, attending parties, and cleaning up afterward, we have little time to actually enjoy the meaning of Christmas.

The first purpose of Christmas is *celebration*! We learn this from the angel's opening statement to the shepherds of Bethlehem. God had wonderful news for us that would cause us all to rejoice, celebrate, and throw a party:

> *"I bring you good news of great joy that will be*
> *for all the people."*
>
> LUKE 2:10 NIV

The good news of Christmas is worth celebrating for three reasons. It is personal: *"I bring YOU."* It is positive: *"GOOD news of great joy."* And it is universal: *"for ALL the people."* It doesn't matter who you are, what you've done, where you've been, or where you're headed—this news is for you.

A national magazine used to carry a feature called "News You Can Use." I always read that section first. The angel brought us news we can use. It's the best news in the world:

God loves you!

God is with you!

God is for you!

CHRISTMAS IS A TIME TO CELEBRATE THAT GOD *LOVES* YOU!

The most famous statement in the Bible is Jesus' explanation of why God sent him to earth: *"God loved the world so much that he gave his one and only Son, so that everyone who believes in him will not perish but have eternal life."*[1]

The entire reason for Christmas is the love of God. God loves you so much that he came to earth as a human so you could get to know him and learn to trust him and love him back. Theologians call this *the Incarnation.* God became one of us, a human being, so we could understand what he is really like.

God has given us, as human beings, the capacity to know him in ways animals can't. He created us *in his image,*[2] which includes the ability to enjoy a personal relationship with him. Then he took the initiative to send Jesus so we could understand his love and our need for him.

Of course, we know a little about God by simply observing his creation. For instance, by looking at nature we know that our Creator loves variety: he created an incredibly diverse universe. Think of the limitless array of plants, animals, rock formations, snowflakes, and people. No two human beings, even twins, are exactly alike. God doesn't make clones or copies. Every one of us is an original. After you were born, God broke the mold.

By surveying natural phenomena, we also know that God is powerful and organized, and that he loves beauty. We all know that God must enjoy watching us enjoy what he's created. Otherwise, why would he give us so many ways to enjoy it? He gave us taste buds, then filled the world with incredible flavors like choco-

late and cinnamon and all the other spices. He gave us eyes to perceive color and then filled the world with a rainbow of shades. He gave us sensitive ears and then filled the world with rhythms and music. Your capacity for enjoyment is evidence of God's love for you. He could have made the world tasteless, colorless, and silent. The Bible says that God "*richly provides us with everything for our enjoyment.*"[3] He didn't have to do it, but he did, because he loves us.

Still, until Jesus arrived, our understanding of God's love was limited. So God invaded earth! It was the greatest invasion in history, and nothing has been the same since. God could have chosen thousands of ways to communicate with us, but since he designed us, he knew the best way to communicate with us would be face-to-face.

If God had wanted to communicate to birds, he would have become a bird. If God had wanted to communicate to cows, he would have become a cow. But God wanted to communicate to us, so he became one

of us. He didn't send an angel or a prophet or a politi-
cian or an ambassador. He came himself. If you really
want people to know how much you love them, you
can't send a representative to communicate it. You have
to say it personally. That's what God did at Christmas.

The Bible tells us that God *is* love. It doesn't say
God *has* love, but God *is* love. Love is the essence of
God's character. It is his very nature. The reason that
everything in the universe exists is because God wanted
to love it. *"The Lord is good to all; he has compassion on
all he has made."*[4]

Think about this. If God didn't want to love something, he would not have created it. Everything you
see, *and the trillions of things you can't see,* was made by
God for his enjoyment. He loves it all, even when we
mess it up with our sin. He still has a purpose for it.
Every star, every planet, every plant, every animal,
every cell, and, most of all, every human being was created out of God's compassion.

You were created as an object of God's love. He made *you* in order to love you! His love is the reason you're alive and breathing and reading this book. Every time your heart beats and every time you take a breath, God is saying, "I love you." You would not exist if God had not wanted you. Although there are accidental parents, there are no accidental babies. The parents may not have planned them, but God did.

Did you know that God was thinking of you even *before* he made the world? In fact, it is why he created it! He designed this planet's environment with just the right characteristics so human beings could live on it. The Bible says, "*God decided to give us life through the word of truth so we might be the most important of all the things he made.*"[5] We matter to God more than anything else he has made.

Because God's love for you is unconditional, he loves you on your bad days as much as on your good days. He loves you when you don't feel his love as much as when you do. He loves you regardless of your performance, your moods, your actions, or your thoughts. His love for you is unchanging. Everything else will change during your lifetime, but God's love for you is constant, steady, and continuous. It's the foundation for unshakable confidence.

There is nothing you can do that will make God stop loving you. You could try, but you'd fail—because God's love for you is based on his character, not your conduct. It's based on who he is, not what you've done. The Bible says, *"Christ's love is greater than anyone can ever know, but I pray that you will be able to know that love."* [6]

One potential problem of our annual Christmas celebrations is that many people only think of Jesus as a baby! Their conception of him is only as a helpless newborn in his mother's arms. If Jesus had never grown up to do what he did, he'd have no power to transform our lives.

But the baby born in Bethlehem did not stay a

baby. Jesus grew to manhood, modeled for us the kind of life that pleases God, taught us the truth, paid for every sin we commit by dying on a cross, then proved that he was God and could save us by coming back to life. This is the Good News. When the Romans nailed Jesus to a cross, they stretched his arms as wide as they could. With his arms wide open, Jesus was physically demonstrating, "I love you this much! I love you so much it hurts! I'd rather die than live without you!" The next time you see a picture or statue of Jesus with outstretched arms on the cross, remember, he is saying, "I love you *this* much!"

CHRISTMAS IS A TIME TO CELEBRATE
THAT GOD IS *WITH* YOU!

A s I mentioned, many people often feel alone at Christmas. Right now, you may not *feel* like God is with you. But God's presence in your life has nothing to do with your feelings. Your emotions are susceptible to all kinds of influences, so they are often unreliable. Sometimes the worst advice you can get is "Do what you feel." Often what we feel is neither real nor right. Your emotional state can be the result of memories, hormones, medicines, food, lack of sleep, tension, or fears. Whenever I start to feel anxious about a situation, I remind myself that fear is often **F**alse **E**vidence **A**ppearing **R**eal.

God came to earth at Christmas to remind you that he

is always with you, no matter where you are. That's a fact, whether you feel it or not. The Bible says, "*I can never escape from your Spirit! I can never get away from your presence!*"[7] But you must connect or "tune in" to his presence on a moment-by-moment basis, and that is a skill that can be learned. I talk about it in my book *The Purpose Driven Life.*

Sometimes babies are given two or three middle names to honor relatives. God commanded that Jesus be given several names to explain his purpose for coming to earth. One of Jesus' names is Immanuel. It means *God is with us.*[8] It's no wonder the angel told the shepherds, "Do not be afraid!" You lose your fear when God is near. God's presence trumps our panic.

You may have been abandoned in life—by a spouse, by your parents, by your children, or by people you thought were friends. Everyone has faced the pain and heartache of rejection in some way. You may have experienced the sting of racial or ethnic prejudice, gender bigotry, or religious intolerance. If so, I am sorry. But God has not abandoned you! He never will! The Bible says, *"God has said, 'I will never leave you; I will never abandon you.'"* [9]

One of God's great promises in the Bible is this: *"When you go through deep waters, I will be with you. When you go through rivers of difficulty, you will not drown. When you walk through the fire of oppression, you will not be burned up; the flames will not consume you."*[10] I don't know what difficulty you feel you're drowning in right now or where the heat is on in your life, but I do know that whatever it is, God knows about it, cares about it, understands it, and is going through it with you. You're not alone. That leads us to a third aspect of God's Good News.

CHRISTMAS IS A TIME TO CELEBRATE
THAT GOD IS *FOR* YOU!

T he phrase "for you" is used often in the Bible. For instance, when Jesus met people, his first words to them were often a question: *"What do you want me to do for you?"*[11] When Jesus instituted communion he said, *"This is my body, which is given for you."*[12] Saint Paul said, *"If God is for us, who can be against us?"*[13] When you're facing a personal attack, it is great to have God *with* you, but it is even greater to know he is *for* you!

Many people feel that God is secretly out to "get" them—that he is constantly playing a game of "Gotcha!" and just waiting for them to mess up and fail so he can say, "I told you so!" They imagine God as some kind of sadistic cosmic grouch who enjoys frustrating our plans and is always looking for ways to criticize, judge, or get even with us. But God himself says otherwise: *"'I know the plans I have for you,' says the Lord. 'They are plans for good and not for disaster, to give you a future and a hope.'"*[14]

No one wants what's best for you more than God. No one knows better what will make you truly happy! God doesn't want you to be afraid of him. He wants you to run *to* him, not *from* him. In fact, 365 times in the Bible, God says, *"Don't be afraid!"* That's one "Fear not" for every day of the year! So what are you afraid of? None of us knows what we'll face this next year, but we can know that God loves us, God is with us, and God is for us. One plus God is a majority in any situation.

So where does our fear of God come from? Primarily two sources: a guilty conscience and ignorance of what God is really like. The Bible says, *"There is no fear in love. But perfect love drives out fear, because fear has to*

do with punishment. The one who fears is not made perfect in love." [15] Guilt makes us insecure.

Have you ever noticed that some people get extremely nervous anytime anyone mentions God or Jesus in a conversation? I've seen people have an instant visceral reaction at the mention of Jesus. Instinctively, their stomachs, faces, and muscles all tighten up with a fight-or-flight response. Maybe you've felt yourself react that way and wondered why. Adrenaline starts rushing through your veins. One common reason is that we all carry secret, hidden guilt from things we've done wrong, and we feel ashamed of ways we've acted and treated others. Assuming that God is mad at us and that he's going to scold us for all the ways we've fallen short, we seek to avoid even talking about him.

But God is not mad at you. He is mad *about* you! Jesus said, *"God did not send his Son into the world to condemn the world, but to save the world."* [16] If you study the life of Jesus, you'll quickly see that when you make a mistake, Jesus doesn't rub it in. He *rubs it out*. He came to erase all your sins, mistakes, failures, and regrets. That's why the first statement the angel made to the shepherds was "*Do not be afraid!*" Jesus came to save us, not to scare us! It's a reason to celebrate.

CELEBRATE CHRISTMAS WITH
A BIRTHDAY PARTY FOR JESUS!

————————

My sister recently found a picture of me as a three-year-old, standing next to a birthday cake for Jesus, complete with candles. The cake was my idea. As a toddler, I asked my mother, "Why do we have Christmas?" Mom patiently explained that Christmas is the celebration of Jesus' birthday. In a burst of preschooler inspiration, I concluded with a child's logic, "Well then, we should have a birthday party! We can have cake and Kool-Aid and sing happy birthday to Jesus!" My mother said, "Okay, we will!"

Thus began a five-decade Warren family tradition, our Birthday Party for Jesus every Christmas Eve, complete with angel food cake and candles that the youngest child

————————

I was almost three years old when I suggested
we have our first birthday party for Jesus.

(and now grandchild) gets to blow out. Four generations now participate in the sharing.

Besides singing carols and reading the Christmas story from the Bible, each family member takes a turn sharing his or her answers to two personal questions:

"What, from this past year, are you thankful to God for?" and, "Since it's Jesus' birthday, what gift will you give him this next year?" These two simple questions have prompted some of the most profound and moving moments in our family's history.

Because of today's pace of life, we quickly forget all the good things God does for us, and we move on to the next challenge. That's why I recommend that you establish an annual celebration, a birthday party for Jesus in your home with family or close friends. Scheduling a once-a-year time to pause and review God's grace in your life and to recommit yourself to knowing and loving him better is a great way to make Christmas more meaningful.

Our party changes each year as our family changes. When my brother, sister, and I were young, the atmosphere was light and fun and full of wiggles. As we matured, our sharing became more intense, even profound. The same cycle repeated itself with our children, and now it is repeating with our grandchildren. We always grow stronger and closer to God and to one another from sharing our hearts and commitments to Christ.

Generations come and go. My parents are now in heaven. But in a world where everything constantly changes, the stability of our family faith in Christ has enabled us to face the inevitable problems of life: cancer, death of loved ones, unemployment, marriage problems, family conflicts, financial difficulties, and all sorts of stresses and strains. No matter what you are going through this Christmas, try celebrating the real thing. It will make a difference.

A TIME FOR

Salvation

When the right time finally came,

God sent his own Son. He came as the

son of a human mother and lived

under the Jewish Law.

GALATIANS 4:4 TEV

Years ago I was sitting in my parked car on a hot summer day waiting for my wife, Kay, to come out of a store. Amy, our daughter, was three years old and strapped into a child's car seat in the back. Frustrated by having to wait in the heat and limited by her car seat, she hung her head out the window and yelled "Please, God! Get me out of this!" She was crying out for a *savior*.

Because she couldn't free herself, my daughter needed someone bigger and more powerful to rescue her from her frustrating predicament. Ever felt like that? We all have. Maybe you're feeling that way this Christmas. You feel like yelling, "Please, God! Get me out of this!"

The second purpose of Christmas is *salvation*!
Salvation is typically defined as deliverance from sin,
self, and hell. It definitely includes all that, but it also
embraces much more. We are not only saved *from*
something bad, we are saved *for* something good. The
Bible says, "*In Christ Jesus, God made us to do good
works, which God planned in advance for us to live our
lives doing.*"[17]

God has a great purpose and a good plan for your
life. Salvation also means being given the freedom and
power to fulfill God's purpose for your life.

The announcement of salvation for anyone in the
world who'd accept it was the angel's second declara-
tion of good news to the shepherds of Bethlehem at
the first Christmas:

> *"Today . . . there has been born for you a
> Savior, who is Christ the Lord."*
>
> LUKE 2:11 NASB

Notice that this savior is "*for you*"! He came for your benefit. Jesus is a *personal* savior. What does that mean? When someone says, "Jesus Christ is my personal savior," or when anyone asks, "Have you been saved?" what are they referring to?

It's likely you haven't given much thought to your need for a savior or what you need to be saved from. In my Christmas-shopper survey, I asked, "What do you need to be saved from?" and the answers I heard varied widely.

- ❖ "From worry"
- ❖ "From the cost of gas and my debt"
- ❖ "From people who've hurt me"
- ❖ "From my anger"
- ❖ "From my past—I can't seem to let it go"
- ❖ "From my bad habits"
- ❖ "From myself"

When people think of spiritual salvation, they often have a very narrow concept of it: they think that salvation is being saved from hell. But God had so much more in mind than just fire insurance when he sent Jesus to be our savior. God's gift of true salvation is freedom, purpose, and life in three dimensions. It includes your past, your present, and your future:

Jesus saves you from something.

Jesus saves you for something.

Jesus saves you by something.

JESUS CAME TO SAVE
YOU *FROM SIN AND YOURSELF*

L et me be blunt: *you* are the source of most of your problems. Even when other people cause you problems, your natural response often makes them worse. You trip yourself up far more often than you realize or would like to admit. If you're honest with yourself, you'll admit that you have habits you can't break, thoughts you don't want, emotions you don't like, insecurities and fears you can't hide, and regrets and resentments you can't let go of, and you say things you later wish you'd never said. Frankly, *you* are the problem with you. For change to happen, it must start in your heart.

We're all born with an "I" problem. We are, by nature, self-centered. Just ask any parent who has raised a child. We don't have to be taught to be selfish. It comes naturally. If people were naturally unselfish, there'd never be any conflict, divorce, abuse, greed, crime, gossip, or war on earth.

Our natural inclination is to want our own way instead of God's way. This tendency to make wrong choices instead of right ones is called *sin*. The middle letter of sin is *I,* and whenever I place myself at the center of my life, I sin. It is any attitude or action that denies God his rightful place as first in my life.

Sin is our greatest problem, and it is universal. You and I sin every day—with our words, our thoughts, and our actions. The Bible says, "*Not a single person on earth is always good and never sins.*"[18] Nobody's perfect. Nobody bats a thousand. No one has a perfect record. God says, "*For all have sinned and fall short of the glory of God.*"[19] I don't measure up to my own imperfect standards, much less God's perfect ones! This is not a popular concept, but then, it is not exactly news either! Unless you are in total denial, you know that you make wrong choices all the time. The Bible says, "*If we claim we have no sin, we are only fooling ourselves and not living in the truth. . . . If we claim we have not sinned, we are calling God a liar.*"[20] I've met tens of thousands of people while traveling the globe, and I've never met a person who claimed to be perfect. *Never.* None of us is sinless, and we know it.

What's worse is that sin is habit forming. The more we do it, the easier it gets. If you've ever tried to break an addiction, maintain a diet, keep a New Year's resolution, or change your life by willpower alone, you know how frustrating that is. You can identify with the apostle Paul's frustration when he wrote, "*I don't understand myself at all, for I really want to do what is right, but I can't. I do what I don't want to—what I hate. I know perfectly well that what I am doing is wrong, and my bad conscience proves that I agree with these laws that I am breaking. But I can't help myself.*"[21]

Our actions, both conscious and unconscious,

shout out, "I don't need God! I want to run my own life, and I want to be my own God. I think I know what's best for me more than God does, so I'm going to do what I feel like doing." Every time you do what you want to do instead of what God tells you to do, you are acting like you are God. That war with God creates enormous conflict and stress in your mind, on your body, and in your relationships.

This attitude of prideful self-will causes you to be disconnected from God and feel distant from him. This focus on self is why you feel that God is a million miles away and that your prayers are just bouncing off the ceiling. If you feel far from God, guess who moved? God didn't. The Bible says, "*The trouble is that your sins have cut you off from God.*" [22]

Our disconnectedness from God, which is due to our stubborn sinfulness, is the source of every single human problem on earth. On a personal level it causes worry, fear, anxiety, confusion, depression, conflict, discouragement, and emptiness. It causes us to act in ways that create guilt, shame, resentment, and regret. You weren't meant to live disconnected from God, so when you do, you feel the tension. You feel spiritually empty.

On a global level, we see the effect of sin all around us: war, injustice, corruption, prejudice, poverty, sex trafficking, and all our other social problems. Even many diseases are caused by our refusal to live by God's standards for healthy living. Who can save us? Not government. Not business. Not academics. These can only deal with the visible symptoms and results of sin. But any lasting solution must start in the heart, and only God can transform hearts.

SALVATION IS FREEDOM

nother word for salvation is "freedom." The Bible says, *"I was in trouble, so I called to the Lord. The Lord answered me and set me free."*[23] From what does Jesus offer to set us free?

Free from *guilt over the past*. Guilt is the mental price we pay for violating our God-given consciences. We know that if we break a law, we have to pay a penalty. When we break God's universal moral laws, someone has to pay for that too. But God, out of his deep love for us, sent Jesus to solve that problem. *"The reward for sin is death, but the gift that God freely gives is everlasting life found in Christ Jesus our Lord."*[24]

When Jesus died on the cross, he paid for everything you've ever done wrong or *ever will do wrong in the future.* How great is that? It has been called the Great Exchange, and you and I get the better end of the deal. *"God took the sinless Christ and poured into him our sins. Then, in exchange, he poured God's goodness into us!"*[25]

God's forgiveness is far more powerful than all of your mistakes and sins put together, so you get a clean slate. That's freedom. Even if there were no heaven or hell (there are), the gift of not having to carry the load of a guilty conscience every day is wonderful.

Free from *bitterness and resentment.* Undoubtedly, you've been hurt by what others have said or done to you in the past. We can't control what others do to us, but we can choose how we respond. Resentment is a cancer of your emotions. Unless you allow Jesus to free you from it, it will eventually destroy your happiness.

Free from the *expectations of others.* How often have you said or done things you didn't want to do simply because you wanted to avoid the disapproval of others? The Bible says, "*The fear of human opinion disables.*"[26] Constantly worrying about what other people think about you is a dangerous trap. It will rob you of confidence, limit your potential, drain your energy, and keep you from becoming all God intends for you to be.

The antidote to fearing disapproval is to build your life on the foundation of God's unconditional love for you. Love liberates. It is a confidence builder. The Bible says, "*There is no fear in love. But perfect love drives out fear, because fear has to do with punishment. The one who fears is not made perfect in love.*"[27]

No matter what you do in life, some people aren't going to like it. And the brighter the light, the more bugs it attracts. When *The Purpose Driven Life* became well known, I became a target of mean-spirited critics who seemed to relish attacking and misrepresenting me. I tried to focus on supporting my wife, Kay, who was battling cancer at that time, but the attacks were discouraging. During that experience, I was encouraged by God's frequent little reminders of his love for me. One weekend, the great London pastor and author John Stott and I were co-preaching a sermon at Saddleback Church. John is a spiritual giant who has been a dear friend and mentor to me. After speaking together, we were having a quiet conversation, and John asked me to write the foreword for *Basic Christianity,* his classic bestseller. I was humbled that he'd want to be publicly associated with me. For weeks, every time I remembered it, I'd think, *Of all the people around the world that John Stott knows and respects, he chose me!* His love for me, and that of other great people I respected, gave me the confidence to ignore the disapproval of people who didn't know me.

Affirmation from others is encouraging, but feeling deeply loved and chosen by God is far greater! The Bible says, "*Even before he made the world, God loved us and chose us in Christ to be holy and without fault in his eyes.*"[28] Did you know that? Before the world was created, God loved you. The Bible often refers to God's decision to love you unconditionally as God's *electing* or *calling* or *choosing* you.

All of us have experienced rejection and carry the scars in our hearts. You undoubtedly remember those painful times in your life. You may recall being made fun of at school by more popular kids or being the last one chosen for a team or receiving hurtful words from a parent or having a friend or spouse walk out of your life. You may have spent years trying to earn the approval of someone who seems unpleasable. Understand this: if you haven't gotten that person's approval by now, it is unlikely you'll ever get it. But the good news is that you don't need any human approval to be happy!

In order to be set free from living for the approval of others, you need to refocus on how much you matter to God and his unconditional love for you. Here are some statements from the Bible to focus on: *"What can we say about such wonderful things as these? If God is for us, who can ever be against us?"*[29] *"Who will bring a charge against God's elect? God is the one who justifies."*[30] *"Even if my father and mother abandon me, the Lord will hold me close."*[31]

So many people base their identity on the judgments and opinions of those around them. But that only leads to greater insecurity. Find your true identity in God, not in what others say about you. In his brilliant book *Jesus of Nazareth,* His Holiness Pope Benedict XVI writes, "Man knows himself only when he learns to understand himself in light of God, and he knows others only when he sees the mystery of God in them." [32]

Free from *addictive habits.* You've probably figured out by now that good intentions and New Year's resolutions are not enough to break out of self-destructive patterns and routines. You tried to change,

but you inevitably reverted back to old ways. With each cycle of best intentions, failure, and remorse, you feel more trapped and hopeless. You need a power greater than yourself. You need a savior! Jesus said, *"If the Son sets you free, then you will be really free!"* [33]

God never intended for you to go through life on your own power. He *wants* you to trust him and depend on him. That's why he allows problems in your life that you have no possible chance of solving on your own. Actually, he had the solution to your problem in mind long before you even knew it was a problem. He's been waiting for you to stop trying and start trusting.

Free from the *fear of death*. The acid test of what you believe is not how you act at weddings and births and graduations. You can pretty much believe anything you want when things are going great. But when the emotional storms of life beat down your dreams, when relational earthquakes rip apart your relationships, when financial fires turn your assets to ashes, when physical pain pummels your body, and when the eventual deaths of loved ones leave you lonely and lost, what will uphold and empower you then? It is foolish to live in denial, unprepared for what everyone knows is inevitable.

As a pastor, I have participated in countless funerals, so I know well the difference that a personal relationship with Jesus makes in how death is handled. I've looked into the eyes of people who have no hope or assurance of heaven, and I've sensed the terror and despair in their hearts at the gravesides. Knowing Jesus makes all the difference in the world when you face death.

If you accept what Jesus did for you on the cross, your eternal destiny will be secured, and you'll no longer fear death. The Bible says, "*Since we, God's children, are human beings—made of flesh and blood—he [Jesus] became flesh and blood too by being born in human form; for only as a human being could he die and in dying break the power of the devil who had the power of death. Only in that way could he deliver those who through fear of death have been living all their lives as slaves to constant dread."* [34]

JESUS CAME TO SAVE YOU *FOR A PURPOSE*

———————

At some point in life, each of us struggles with three basic questions. The first is the question of existence: why am I alive? The second is the question of significance: does my life matter? And the third is the question of intention: what is my purpose?

God has never created anything without a purpose. Since you are alive, you can be certain that God has a purpose for your life. The Bible says, "*Long before he laid down earth's foundations, he had us in mind, had settled on us as the focus of his love.*" [35] But here's the problem: every one of us has strayed from God's intended purposes for our lives. Like a train that has jumped off the tracks, we've been derailed by our own stubbornness and sinful choices. The Bible says, "*We're all like sheep*

———————

who've wandered off and gotten lost. We've all done our own thing, gone our own way. And God has piled all our sins, everything we've done wrong, on him [Jesus]." [36]

Although God created each of us for a purpose, we've all taken many detours in life, thinking we knew better. So God had to send Jesus as our savior—to redeem us from sin, to reset the directions of our lives, and to restore us to his original purposes for our lives. We are not just saved *from* evil; we're saved *for* good! *"[Jesus] died for all so that all who live—having received eternal life from him—might live no longer for themselves, to please themselves, but to spend their lives pleasing Christ who died and rose again for them."* [37]

For more than thirty years, my life verse has been Acts 13:36: David served God's purpose in his generation, then he died. This phrase, "he served God's purpose in his generation," is the ultimate definition of a life well lived. You use your life to do that which is timeless and eternal (God's purpose) in a timely and contemporary way (in your generation). You serve that which never changes (God's Word) in a setting that is constantly changing (the world). This is what it means to live a *purpose-driven life,* and there is no greater adventure, nothing more fulfilling, no better way to leave a lasting legacy with your life.

Imagine that phrase written on *your* gravestone. My prayer is that others will be able to say that about you when you die—that you served God's purpose in your generation. There is no better description of success.

God creates you, shapes you, gifts you, calls you, and saves you for a purpose. That's why the Bible says, "*Give yourselves completely to God—every part of you— for you are back from death and you want to be tools in the hands of God, to be used for his good purposes.*"[38] Nothing compares to the thrill of being used by God for a great purpose. It is the deepest longing in your heart, and no other experience can take the place of it. It is why you were created.

In *The Purpose Driven Life* I explained that everyone lives at one of three levels: survival, success, or significance. Most of the world lives at the survival level. Half of the world's six billion people live on less than two dollars a day. Over one billion live on less than one dollar a day. That's the survival level.

If you live in the United States, you live at the success level, even if you feel poor. Most of the world would love to have our problems. But success doesn't satisfy. You can have a lot to live on and still have nothing to live for. You can be so busy making a living that you fail to make a life.

You were made for far more than success. You were created for significance. But you'll never find significance in possessions, pleasures, or positions. Significance comes from service—giving your life away for a purpose greater than yourself. Jesus said, "*If you insist on saving your life, you will lose it. Only those who throw away their lives for my sake and for the sake of the Good News will ever know what it means to really live.*" [39]

When you finally begin fulfilling the purpose that God created you for and Jesus saves you for, you realize, "This is my niche! This is why I am alive! This is my reason for being. Now I know why I exist." All the success in the world will never give you that deep satisfaction. There will always be a hole in your heart because you were made to know, love, trust, and serve God.

So let me ask you two very pointed questions: Knowing that nothing else you've tried has completely satisfied that longing in your soul, what are you waiting for? Why not accept Jesus as your savior? You get your past forgiven, you get a purpose for living, and you get a home in heaven. No one else can make that kind of offer. Only God can.

JESUS CAME TO SAVE YOU *BY HIS GRACE*

In practically every area of life—school, sports, work—we are judged by our performance. The American work ethic is built on effort, sweat, competition, and hard work. Growing up, Americans are taught that there's no such thing as a free lunch; you get what you pay for; if it's to be, it's up to me; if you want something done right, do it yourself; and God helps those who help themselves.

So when it comes to spiritual matters, many assume God relates to us on the same performance-based ethic. You may feel that you have to earn God's approval, deserve God's love, and work your way to heaven by doing good or trying to be perfect. If you've thought that, I've got good news for you: that's not at all how it works! Here's what the Bible says about what you must do to be saved: *"The people asked Jesus, 'What are the things God wants us to do?' Jesus answered, 'The work God wants you to do is this: Believe the One he sent.'"*[40] Salvation is not a matter of trying, but trusting. It's not a matter of proving you deserve it, but accepting it by faith, knowing you don't deserve it.

The idea of grace is so foreign and antithetical to the popular misconceptions about God and even other religions that when the Bible talks about salvation as a free gift of God's grace, many people respond with a blank stare. There is a mental and emotional disconnect. We are so used to receiving conditional love ("I will love you *if* . . ." or "I love you *because* . . .") that unconditional grace is an unfamiliar and even uncomfortable concept.

Religion is man's attempt to please God. Grace is God reaching down to man. Every religion boils down to one word: "do!" Do our list of things, and you will earn God's love. Each religion has its own unique list of rules, and if you compare the lists, you discover they are often contradictory. But the big idea behind all religions is that you must work, strive, and put forth great effort in order to get God to like you.

So God came to earth as Jesus essentially to say: "You guys have got it all wrong! Of course doing good things matters, but it doesn't make me love you any more or any less. My love for you is unlimited, unconditional, unchanging, and undeserved. So let me teach you a new concept called grace. You can't purchase it, work for it, or be good enough to merit it. It's a gift that will cost me a lot, but it is free to you. Everything I do for you, to you, in you, and through you—every single blessing you have in life—is a gift of my grace. I've done it all for you."

While religions are based on the word "do," salvation is based on the word "done." When Jesus died for you on the cross, he exclaimed, "*It is finished!*"[41] It's

extremely important to note that Jesus didn't say, "*I am finished,*" because he wasn't! He had more to do. Three days later, he came back to life, resurrected from death, and walked around Jerusalem for forty days. He met with individuals and groups of up to five hundred people before ascending back to heaven.

So what was finished? The payment for your salvation! The phrase "it is finished" is actually a single word in Hebrew that Jesus cried out. It was stamped on bills that had been paid off and on prison sentences that had been completed. It meant "paid in full!" Religion says, "do!" Jesus says, "done!" He has already taken care of the expense of your salvation.

Years ago, a guy asked me, "What must I do to get to heaven?" I shocked him by replying, "You're too late." He didn't expect that answer and anxiously responded, "What do you mean, it's too late to do anything?" I said, "What needed to be done was done for you two thousand years ago by Jesus. All you need to do is accept what he's already done for you! There's nothing more to add. It's grace plus nothing."

The Bible says, "*It is by grace you have been saved, through faith—and this not from yourselves, it is the gift of God—not by works, so that no one can boast.*"[42] Notice that your Christmas gift from God comes *by* grace and *through* faith.

BY GRACE

hat is grace? Grace is God's love in action. Grace is when God freely gives you what you need even though you don't deserve it and can never repay him. Grace is when God solves your greatest problem before you even know it is a problem. Grace is the face of God when he looks at your faults, failures, and fears. Grace is God's Riches At Christ's Expense.

God says, "I know that you've failed to measure up to my perfect standard. *For everyone has sinned; we all fall short of God's glorious standard.*[43] And since heaven wouldn't be a perfect place anymore if I filled it with sinful, imperfect people, there's no way I can allow you into heaven unless I solve your greatest problem—one you can't solve by yourself. You need forgiveness and a total makeover. So here's my plan: I will come to earth as a human being, and I will sacrifice myself in love to pay off the massive debt you owe because of your sin and the damage it has done." The Bible tells us, "*He canceled the debt, which listed all the rules we failed to follow. He took away that record with its rules and nailed it to the cross.*"[44]

Christmas would have no meaning if Jesus hadn't died on the cross for us and then proved that he is God by rising again three days later on Easter Sunday. *"He [Jesus] is the atoning sacrifice for our sins, and not only for ours but also for the sins of the whole world."*[45] By dying to save you, Jesus paid off your debt, compensated for the damages of your sin, redeemed you from slavery to evil, and substituted himself to take the punishment you deserved. That, my friend, is what people are singing about when they sing "Amazing Grace"!

You may be privileged to feel deeply loved by others, or you may feel completely unloved this Christmas. Regardless, you need to think about this: no man or woman will ever love you as completely and deeply as Jesus does. His death for you proves it. *"This is love: not that we loved God, but that he loved us and sent his Son as an atoning sacrifice for our sins."*[46] The better you understand what Jesus did on the cross, the more you'll understand what life is really all about.

Do you know why the tradition of gift giving at Christmas began? Because God gave the first and greatest gift at the first Christmas—the gift of his Son. *"Thanks be to God for his indescribable gift!"*[47]

Our world is filled with frustrated people who don't know what they are looking for and wouldn't know where to find it if they did. They just know that something is missing, something is incomplete in their lives. It's a gnawing feeling that there's got to be more to life than a paycheck until retirement. Maybe you have tried to find fulfillment in status or sex or salary or security or success, to no avail. What you're missing—

"A Savior has been born to you;

he is Christ the Lord!"

what you *really* need—is salvation. You were made by God and for God, and until you understand that, life will never make sense.

You may be looking for a savior in the wrong places: *If I could just find the right man or woman, everything would be great. If I had a certain job or got a promotion or had a baby or attained a certain level of wealth, then I'd feel peaceful and fulfilled. If only I could achieve a beautiful body, impress the right people, own the right things, or escape to Tahiti, then my emptiness would be filled.*

The answer is not in a place, a program, or a pill. The answer is a person. It's Jesus. What you're missing is a relationship with the One who created you so he could love you. *"For as you know him better, he will give you, through his great power, everything you need for living a truly good life: he even shares his own glory and his own goodness with us!"*[48]

THROUGH FAITH

God also tells us, "*People are declared righteous because of their faith, not because of their work.*"[49] The theological term for the phrase "declared righteous because of their faith" is "justified." To be justified by God means to be made "just-as-if I'd" never sinned! The warrant for your arrest is cancelled. The charges are dropped. The slate is cleaned. The guilt is gone. The penalty has been paid. Like an old Etch A Sketch turned upside down and shaken or a computer hard drive that has been completely erased of data, the evidence of all your sins and mistakes is wiped out. And how does this great justification happen? Through faith.

Just as parents deeply desire and long for their children to trust their love, God wants you to learn to trust him. The Bible says, "*Without faith it is impossible to please God, because anyone who comes to him must believe that he exists and that he rewards those who earnestly seek him.*"[50] Faith makes God smile. It's not what you do, but whom you trust, that gets you into heaven.

As a young man, I was a lifeguard for three summers. People panic when they sense they are drowning and typically flail their arms around, grasping for anything. Every lifeguard knows that if he tries to rescue someone who's still full of adrenaline and fearfully trying to save himself, the victim will likely pull the lifeguard underwater with him. An experienced lifeguard knows he may have to stay back a foot, tread water, and wait until the drowning person gives up. Then it becomes quite easy to make the rescue. When the victim finally gives up, he relaxes, and the lifeguard can take over. At that point the lifeguard simply puts his arm over the victim and swims back to shore. All the drowning person has to do is trust the lifeguard. But a person can't be saved until he gives up trying to save himself.

Have you given up trying to save yourself? Consider this: if it were possible for you to save yourself and you didn't really need a savior, God would not have wasted the enormous energy, effort, and pain to send one. If there were any other way, don't you think Jesus would have chosen it instead of suffering on a cross?

I have no idea what worries or anxieties or fears you're carrying right now as you are reading this. But Jesus knows, he cares, and he can help you—if you will trust him completely. And he *will* help. Jesus said this: *"Do not be worried and upset. . . . Believe in God and believe also in me."*[51]

God is waiting to save you. He wants to save you *from* sin and self, save you *for* his purpose, and save you *by* his grace, through faith. But you've got to relax, quit trying to save yourself, let go, and trust your savior to do it for you.

Years ago I was visiting my dear friend Peter Drucker at his home. Peter was a true Renaissance man, the father of modern management and one of the most brilliant thinkers of the twentieth century. I asked Peter, "How did you come to accept Jesus Christ as your savior?" He thought about it for a few seconds, then replied, "The day that I finally understood grace, I realized I was never going to get a better deal than that!"

When Jesus was on the cross paying for our sins, the skeptics standing around mocked and taunted him, saying, "*If you are the Son of God, save yourself and come down from the cross!*"[52] Of course, Jesus ignored them, because that wasn't his purpose in coming to earth. He didn't come to save *himself*. He came to save *you*.

What have you got to lose by saying yes to Jesus? You'll lose guilt, insecurity, lack of purpose, fear of death, hopelessness, anxiety, shame, powerlessness, and a lot of other baggage that you carry when you attempt to live without God's guidance. Who would turn down an offer like that? Still, God gives you the choice. You can decide to keep living a self-centered life, separated from God, or you can choose to turn your mind and heart from going your own way to following Jesus (that's called *repentance*). Then ask for forgiveness for all your sins, and put your trust in God's Son, Jesus, and what he has already done for you!

A TIME FOR

Reconciliation

Now we rejoice in our wonderful new

relationship with God —

all because of what our

Lord Jesus Christ has done . . .

making us friends of God.

ROMANS 5:11 TLB

Much of world history is the story of conflict. During the past 5,560 years there have been nearly 15,000 wars, and these are only the ones we know about. As I write this, there are thirty-two large and small wars going on in the world. We human beings don't seem to be very good at living in peace with one another. We're much better at disagreeing, fighting, and feuding. A hundred years ago, popular sentiment believed that if we could just get the world educated, all the wars would vanish. But after two world wars occurred among the most educated nations on the planet, that naive optimism has vanished. Without a transformation of the heart, education simply allows us to think up more sophisticated ways to kill one another. There are many brilliant people in prison. An educated mind does not automatically produce a peaceful heart. What the world desperately needs is *reconciliation*.

Reconciliation is the restoration of peace. Peace with God, peace with others, and peace in your own heart. It is the powerful miracle cure for broken lives and relationships. Reconciliation defuses conflict and turns chaos into calmness. It quiets quarrels. It swaps your stress for God's serenity, turns tension into tranquility, and produces peace of mind instead of panic or pressure. But the spirit of reconciliation seems to be in short supply today.

Fortunately the third purpose of Christmas is *reconciliation*! To the shepherds of Bethlehem, the third announcement of the angel concerned the arrival of the *"Prince of Peace."* [53] Jesus would not only teach the way to peace but would empower us to live lives of peace if we would trust him.

> *"Glory to God in the highest,*
> *and on earth peace,*
> *good will toward men."*
>
> LUKE 2:14 KJV

Last year, I logged about seventy-five thousand miles in international travel. In every country I visited, I witnessed the universal problem of conflict. You can find it in backwater rural areas as well as in high-tech cosmopolitan cities. Economic wealth seems to make no difference at all. In some ways technology is a culprit in the polarization of civilization. The Internet has allowed the formation of millions of micro-subgroups. Niche identities keep getting smaller and smaller.

With the media always playing up our differences

to create entertaining stories, civilization is fast losing its civility. Rudeness, not kindness, is on the increase. In my travels I've observed every imaginable type of conflict—between races, nationalities, language and religious groups, political and ethnic parties, and rich and poor. Then, as a pastor in my community, I constantly deal with interpersonal conflicts in marriages, families, offices, neighborhoods, Little League, and between church members. Then I go home and, like every other family, sometimes have big disagreements there.

The sad result of all this conflict is that the world is littered with the debris of divided homes, damaged children, discarded friendships, and destroyed partnerships. In my Christmas mall survey I asked shoppers, "Where would you like to see peace this Christmas?" Here's what I heard:

❖ "I'd like peace with my parents, my ex, and my kids."

❖ "I'd like to see the end of political bickering on TV."

❖ "I need peace in my mind and my heart."

❖ "A peaceful neighborhood. End prejudice against Muslims."

❖ "If people were more peaceful, maybe they wouldn't be so rude."

❖ "Honestly, if we don't find peace soon, my marriage will be over."

❖ "I want my mom and daddy to get back together."

❖ "I'd like to see peace everywhere."

Is peace on earth really possible, or is it an unattainable fantasy? Is civility—*"good will toward men"*—possible when current culture conditions us to be cynical and sarcastic, to use put-downs and name-calling, to demean and demonize those who believe differently?

The starting point to peace in your life is understanding the causes of conflict. There are many reasons, but here are two big ones. The first is our natural self-centeredness. When I want everything my way, and you want it your way, then my agenda clashes with yours. If neither of us is willing to compromise out of love, sparks fly. This scenario plays out millions of times a day in relationships. Even when you love someone, it doesn't mean you're going to agree on everything. Kay and I learned that on our honeymoon! So the very first Bible verse we memorized together as newlyweds was Proverbs 13:10: *"Only by pride cometh contention."*[54] We needed that verse a lot!

A second common, but less understood, cause of conflict is expecting others to meet needs in our lives that only God can meet. We make demands of others instead of looking to God. So many people get married with unrealistic expectations and then divorce. No human being can fully meet all your needs. That's a job for God.

Instead of complaining and blaming others for your unmet needs, the Bible recommends asking God instead. It says, "*What causes fights and quarrels among you? Don't they come from your desires that battle within you? You want something but don't get it. You kill and covet, but you cannot have what you want. You quarrel and fight. You do not have, because you do not ask God.*" [55] If you prayed as much as you complain and quarrel, you'd have a lot less to argue about and much more peace of mind.

Years ago a friend invited me to attend a stress-management seminar with him. One of the suggestions the instructor gave for stress relief was "Unload your stress by telling it to an unconditional listener." Then he quickly added, "The best way to do this is to talk to your pet!" I sat there amazed that people were actually paying to hear someone suggest that they should have a heart-to-heart with their hamster! Pets are great, but they can't help you resolve the conflicts in your life that are the roots of your stress.

The apostle Paul had a much better alternative: *"Do not worry about anything, but pray and ask God for everything you need, always giving thanks. And God's peace, which is so great we cannot understand it, will keep your hearts and minds in Christ Jesus."*[56]

The reality is that there will never be peace in the world until there's peace within nations. And there will never be peace in our nation until there's peace in our communities. There won't be peace in our communities until there's peace in our families. And there won't be peace in our families until there's peace in our individual lives. That won't happen until the Prince of Peace reigns in our hearts. Jesus came at Christmas to bring to us three kinds of peace:

Peace with God

The peace of God

Peace with others

JESUS OFFERS YOU *PEACE WITH GOD*

You may have never realized that if you're trying to live your way instead of God's way, you're in conflict with God. He created you to live for his purposes, but you've been living in rebellion against God. The Bible says this is a universal problem: *"We're all like sheep who've wandered off and gotten lost. We've all done our own thing, gone our own way. And God has piled all our sins, everything we've done wrong, on him, on him [Jesus]."*[57] It is this unspoken war with God—where each of us chooses to disobey what God has told us to do—that causes tension in your mind and fatigue in your body.

The symptoms of being at war with God are easy to spot: irritability, a quick temper, insecurity, impatience, manipulation, arrogance and boasting, holding grudges, and many other attitudes and habits that the Bible calls the *"works of the flesh."* *The Message* translation of the Bible gives this paraphrase: *"It is obvious what kind of life develops out of trying to get your own way all the time: repetitive, loveless, cheap sex; a stinking accumulation of mental and emotional garbage; frenzied and joyless grabs for happiness . . . cutthroat competition; all-consuming-yet-never-satisfied wants; a brutal temper; an impotence to love or be loved; divided homes and divided lives . . . the vicious habit of depersonalizing everyone into a rival; . . . uncontrollable addictions."*[58]

In contrast, the effects of being reconciled to God—being at peace with him—are all the qualities you'd like to have in your life. The Bible calls these the *"fruit of the Spirit"*: *"When the Holy Spirit controls our lives he will produce this kind of fruit in us: love, joy, peace, patience, kindness, goodness, faithfulness, gentleness, and self-control."*[59]

Having counseled many people, I've noticed that there is a built-in longing inside each of us to be at peace with our physical fathers. This desire for connection is hardwired into us. Even if your father has been apathetic toward you or abandoned you or even abused you, something feels missing if that relationship is disconnected. We want it to be different, and we long to be reconciled. People do all kinds of stupid things in an attempt to earn the approval of a parent. It's a deep need.

But an even deeper, unconscious need is to be reconciled and reconnected to your Creator, your heavenly Father. People often tell me they sense an incompleteness in their lives, but they don't know what they're looking for. "Something is missing," they say, or, "There's got to be more to life than just this!" So they try all kinds of remedies—activities, achievements, drugs, affairs—in an attempt to plug the holes in their hearts. What they need is to be reconciled to God.

"I bring you good news of great joy
that will be for all the people."

LUKE 2:10 NIV

Nothing else can compensate for a broken relationship with God.

The good news of Christmas is that Jesus came to be the bridge of reconciliation between you and God. The Bible says, "*God was in Christ, making peace between the world and himself. In Christ, God did not hold the world guilty of its sins.*" [60] It also says, "*Even when we were God's enemies, he made peace with us, because his Son died for us. Yet something even greater than friendship is ours. Now that we are at peace with God, we will be saved by his Son's life.*" [61]

How can you, an imperfect person, be reconciled to a perfect God? Well, it's not a matter of compromise or bargaining or negotiating with God. Peace comes from surrender—total, unconditional surrender to God. You admit that God is God and you are not! You give up the ridiculous notion that you know more about what's best for you and what will make you happy than your Creator does. You give up the rebellious attitude that you can pick and choose which of God's rules you'll follow and which ones you'll ignore.

Why should you surrender to God? Well, one fact is certain: there's no way you can win a war against God. As the title of the 1980s Broadway play points out, "Your arms are too short to box with God!" As Job's friend said, *"Stop quarreling with God! If you agree with him, you will have peace at last, and things will go well for you."* [62]

JESUS OFFERS YOU *THE PEACE OF GOD*

Once you make peace with God, you'll begin to experience the peace *of* God in your heart and in your mind. The more you pray, the less you'll panic. The more you worship, the less you worry. You'll feel more patient and less pressured. The Bible promises, *"You, Lord, give true peace to those who depend on you, because they trust you."* [63]

What robs you of your peace? Most of the culprits fall into one of three categories: uncontrollable circumstances (like illnesses, deaths, and layoffs), unchangeable people (who refuse to cooperate with your plan to change them), and unexplainable problems (when life seems unfair). People respond to these peace robbers in one of three ways: They try harder to control everything, but they're guaranteed to fail at that. They simply give up with a fatalistic attitude, feeling controlled by their circumstances. Or they gain true peace of mind by responding to situations the way Jesus did and depending on his Spirit to empower them to do that.

You've probably heard of the Serenity Prayer, which was made famous by Reinhold Niebuhr, but you may have not read the entire prayer. The first third of the prayer is often quoted and written on posters. But to experience the serenity mentioned in the first third of the prayer, you need to follow the steps laid out in the rest of the prayer:

God grant me the serenity to accept the things
I cannot change; courage to change the things
I can; and wisdom to know the difference.
Living one day at a time; enjoying one
moment at a time; accepting hardships as the

pathway to peace; taking, as He did, this
sinful world as it is, not as I would have it;
trusting that He will make all things right
if I surrender to His Will; that I may be
reasonably happy in this life and supremely
happy with Him forever in the next.

The path to the peace of God comes through living and enjoying one day at a time, accepting what cannot be changed instead of worrying about it, trusting in God's loving care and wisdom, and surrendering to his purpose and plan for your life. Jesus makes this promise: *"Come to me, all of you who are weary and carry heavy burdens, and I will give you rest. Take my yoke upon you. Let me teach you, because I am humble and gentle at heart, and you will find rest for your souls."*[64]

JESUS SHOWS YOU HOW
TO *MAKE PEACE WITH OTHERS*

———————

Once you've made peace *with* God and you begin to experience the peace *of* God in your heart, God wants you to experience the joy of being at peace with all the people in your life. He does this by turning you into a peacemaker. He gives you the desire, then the ability and power, to reconcile with the people in your life with whom you've had conflicts. *"All this comes from the God who settled the relationship between us and him, and then called us to settle our relationships with each other."*[65] When Christ comes into your life, one of the first areas where you see a difference is in your relationships.

Would you like God's blessing on your life and

———————

career? Jesus said, "*Blessed are the peacemakers, for they will be called sons of God.*" [66] Anytime you attempt to restore a broken relationship, you're doing what God would do. And when you help bring other people together who have been estranged from one another, you are acting like Christ. The Bible calls it "*the ministry of reconciliation.*" God looks down on you and says, "That's my girl!" or, "That's my boy! They are doing what I'd do." The true children of God are peacemakers, not troublemakers.

Notice Jesus didn't say, "Blessed are the peace lovers," because everyone *loves* peace. Neither did he say, "Blessed are the peaceable," who are never disturbed by anything. Jesus said, "*Blessed are the peacemakers.*"

What does it mean to be a peacemaker? It's not avoiding conflict. It's not running from a problem or pretending it doesn't exist. When someone says, "I don't want to talk about it," that's cowardice, not peacemaking. When you delay dealing with a conflict, it only grows larger or deeper. Peacemaking is not appeasement either. Always giving in and allowing other people to get their way is passivity, not peacemaking. Jesus never said you must be a doormat or a chameleon and lose your identity. In fact, Jesus never allowed others to define him.

To work for peace means you actively seek to end conflicts, you take the initiative in promoting reconciliation when relationships break down, and you offer forgiveness to those who have hurt you. You pass on to others the same grace that God has shown to you. You bring people together instead of dividing them. *"Those who are peacemakers will plant seeds of peace and reap a harvest of righteousness."*[67]

Many people are reluctant to reconcile strained relationships because they don't understand the difference between forgiveness and trust or the difference between reconciliation and resolution. They are

afraid that if they reconcile, they'll have to return to a hurtful or dysfunctional relationship without any change taking place. That's a misunderstanding of reconciliation.

First of all, reconciliation is not the same as resolution. Reconciliation ends hostility. It doesn't mean you've resolved all the problems in the relationship. You bury the hatchet but not the issues. You continue to talk about the issues and work on them, but now you do it with respect and love instead of sarcasm and anger. You can disagree agreeably. Reconciliation focuses on the relationship, while resolution focuses on the problem. Always focus on reconciliation first. When you do that, the problem shrinks in size and sometimes becomes insignificant or solves itself.

Second, there is a big difference between forgiveness and trust. Forgiveness is to be instant and free. We offer it to others in the same way that God forgave us. We forgive so we can get on with our lives instead of

THE PURPOSE OF CHRISTMAS

getting stuck in the past due to resentment and bitterness. We also remember that Jesus said, "*If you refuse to forgive others, your Father will not forgive your sins.*" [68] But restoring trust is a different matter. Forgiveness takes care of the past. Trust is all about the future, and it must be earned over time. Trust can be lost in a second, but it takes a long time to rebuild it. If you've been in a physically abusive relationship, God expects you to forgive that person so bitterness won't poison your life. But God does not expect you to continue being abused.

Here are some simple steps for being a peacemaker:

❖ Plan a peace conference, taking the initiative.

❖ Empathize with others' feelings, listening to show you care.

❖ Attack the problem, not the person, speaking the truth in love.

❖ Cooperate wherever possible, looking for common ground.

❖ Emphasize reconciliation, not resolution.

Are you allowing people who have hurt you in the past to continue to hurt you now? Every time you rehearse and replay in your mind what happened, you allow them to hurt you again. That's dumb. The Bible says, "*You are only hurting yourself with your anger.*" [69] Resentment is self-destructive because it always hurts you most, and it prolongs your pain. While the people who hurt you go on with their lives, resentment causes you to get stuck in the past. You need to let it go.

Christmas, the season of "*peace on earth, good will toward men,*" is the perfect time to offer the gift of grace to others, while celebrating the grace God has shown you. Who do you need to make peace with this Christmas? You may be thinking, *I could never forgive that person. The memories are too painful and the hurt too deep. I can't just let it go.* That's why you need Jesus as your savior. Only when you feel fully forgiven yourself will you be able to forgive those who've hurt you most. Only as you are filled with the love of Jesus will you be able to let your hurts go and get on with your life.

UNWRAPPING YOUR CHRISTMAS GIFT

I f you sacrificed all you had to buy me a priceless and personalized Christmas gift and I never took the time to unwrap and open it, how would you feel? You'd be disappointed, hurt, and angry at my callous rejection of your generous love. And for me, the gift would be worthless if I left it wrapped and sitting in the corner. There would be zero benefit to me.

It is astounding that so many people have celebrated Christmas every year of their lives without ever having opened their greatest and most expensive Christmas gift. Jesus Christ is God's Christmas gift to you. Wrapped up in Jesus are all the benefits and blessings mentioned in this book—and so much more! In Jesus, your past is forgiven, you get a purpose for living, and you get a home in heaven. Why celebrate Christmas if you're not going to open the best gift of all?

The name Jesus actually means "God saves."[70] Right now, Jesus says this to you: "I can replace the frustration in your heart with peace. I can replace your guilt and shame with forgiveness. I can replace your worry and anxiety with confidence. I can replace your depression with real hope. I can fill your emptiness with meaning and purpose. If you'll trust me completely, I can replace your confusion with clarity. But I'm not going to break down the door of your heart. You've got to invite me in." Aren't you ready to do that?

It doesn't matter whether you are Catholic, Protestant, Jewish, Muslim, Buddhist, Hindu, Mormon, or have no religious background at all. God didn't send Jesus to bring us religion! He came to make a relationship with God possible. *"Now we rejoice in our wonder-*

ful new relationship with God—all because of what our Lord Jesus Christ has done for us in dying for our sins— making us friends of God."[71]

Many years ago, I prayed a simple prayer of commitment that changed my life. I've written it out on page 121, and I hope you'll make it your prayer to God too. But first I want to pray for you.

MY PRAYER FOR YOU

Father, as I write these words, I am praying for everyone who will read them. I don't know the circumstances they are facing right now, but you do know. You know every detail of their lives up to this very moment, and you love them deeply. Thank you for creating them, for loving them, and for sending Jesus to be their savior. You planned this moment before they were born, so I know that you will hear the prayer they are about to pray. Thank you, Lord.

Now I invite you to experience the purposes of Christmas by reading the following prayer as your own. The Bible says, "*It makes no difference who you are or where you're from—if you want God and are ready to do as he says, the door is open.*"[72] If you are by yourself, I strongly encourage you to read it twice—first silently, then aloud.

YOUR CHRISTMAS PRAYER

*Dear God, thank you for sending your Son,
Jesus, so I could get to know you. Thank you
for loving me. Thank you for being with me
all my life even when I didn't know it. I realize I need a savior to set me free from sin,
from myself, and from all the habits, hurts,
and hang-ups that mess up my life. I ask you
to forgive me for my sins. I want to repent and
live the way you created me to live. Be the
Lord of my life, and save me by your grace.
Save me from my sins, and save me for your
purpose. I want to learn to love you, trust you,
and become what you made me to be. Thank
you for creating me and choosing me to be*

part of your family. Right now, by faith, I
accept the Christmas gift of your Son. Fill me
with your peace and assurance so I can be a
peacemaker, and help me share this message of
peace with others. In your name I pray, amen.

When you read that, did you sincerely mean it as a prayer to God? If you did, congratulations! Welcome to the family of God! The Bible says there is joy in heaven[73] anytime anyone commits his or her life to Jesus. If you just now accepted the gift of God's grace by faith, the angels are having a party in heaven for you, *right now*!

WHAT SHOULD I DO NOW?

The first thing you should do is tell others about your decision to give your life to Christ! If they ask, "What does that mean?" hand them this book! You might consider holding a birthday party for Jesus to share your news there. If you've committed your life to Jesus Christ as a result of reading this book, please let me know. I'll help you find a good church home if you don't have one, I'll send you some materials that will help you start growing spiritually, and I'll give you a free subscription to my daily inspirational e-mail. E-mail your story to me at:

rick@thepeaceplan.com

A second step is to begin attending a Bible-teaching church. If you don't have a Bible, they can tell you where to get one. They can also help you be baptized as your public expression of faith. If you e-mail me, I'll do my best to recommend a good church in your area.

A third step is to share the message of peace with others. Pass this book on to a friend. You might give copies of it as Christmas gifts. The greatest gift you can give to anyone is to introduce them to the Good News!

Finally, look for practical ways that you can promote *"peace on earth and good will toward men."* I'd love to send you information on the P.E.A.C.E. Plan that we've been developing. It's a personal, local, and global strategy through which ordinary people are making a difference together wherever they are. P.E.A.C.E. stands for **P**romote reconciliation, **E**quip servant leaders, **A**ssist the poor, **C**are for the sick, and **E**ducate the next generation. You are needed and you can make a difference with your life as a P.E.A.C.E. Partner or P.E.A.C.E. Professional.

Email rick@the peaceplan.com for information and visit www.thepeace plan.com.

For other Purpose Driven resources visit www.saddlebackresources.com.

Merry Christmas!

HOLD A BIRTHDAY PARTY
FOR JESUS THIS CHRISTMAS

Agenda

❖ Sing some Christmas carols.

❖ Read the Christmas story from the Bible, Luke
   2:1–20; Matthew 2:1–12.

❖ Each person shares answers to two questions:

   1. What am I thankful to God for this year?

   2. What am I going to give Jesus for his
      birthday?

❖ Close by praying for one another.

NOTES

1. John 3:16 NLT
2. See Genesis 1:26
3. 1 Timothy 6:17 NIV
4. Psalm 145:9 NIV
5. James 1:18 NCV
6. Ephesians 3:19 NCV
7. Psalm 139:7 NLT
8. See Matthew 1:23
9. Hebrews 13:5 TEV
10. Isaiah 43:2 NLT
11. Matthew 20:32 NIV; also Mark 10:36, 51 NIV
12. 1 Corinthians 11:24 NLT
13. Romans 8:31 NIV
14. Jeremiah 29:11 NLT
15. 1 John 4:18 NIV
16. John 3:17 NLT
17. Ephesians 2:10 NCV
18. Ecclesiastes 7:20 NLT
19. Romans 3:23 NIV
20. 1 John 1:8–10 NLT
21. Romans 7:15–17 TLB
22. Isaiah 59:2 TLB
23. Psalm 118:5 NCV
24. Romans 6:23 GW
25. 2 Corinthians 5:21 TLB
26. Proverbs 29:25 *The Message*
27. 1 John 4:18 NIV
28. Ephesians 1:4 NLT
29. Romans 8:31 NLT
30. Romans 8:33 NASB
31. Psalm 27:10 NLT
32. Pope Benedict XVI, *Jesus of Nazareth* (Garden City, NY: Doubleday), 2007, 282
33. John 8:36 TEV
34. Hebrews 2:14–15 TLB

35. Ephesians 1:4 *The Message*
36. Isaiah 53:6 *The Message*
37. 2 Corinthians 5:15 TLB
38. Romans 6:13 TLB
39. Mark 8:35 TLB
40. John 6:28–29 NCV
41. John 19:30 NIV
42. Ephesians 2:8–9 NIV
43. Romans 3:23 NLT
44. Colossians 2:14 NCV
45. 1 John 2:2 NIV
46. 1 John 4:10 NIV
47. 2 Corinthians 9:15 NIV
48. 2 Peter 1:3 TLB
49. See Romans 4:5
50. Hebrews 11:6 NIV
51. John 14:1 TEV
52. Matthew 27:40 NLT
53. Isaiah 9:6 NIV
54. KJV
55. James 4:1–2 NIV
56. Philippians 4:6–7 NCV
57. Isaiah 53:6 *The Message*
58. Galatians 5:19–21 *The Message*
59. Galatians 5:22–23 TLB
60. 2 Corinthians 5:19 NCV
61. Romans 5:10 CEV
62. See Job 22:21
63. Isaiah 26:3 NCV
64. Matthew 11:28–29 NLT
65. 2 Corinthians 5:18 *The Message*
66. Matthew 5:9 NIV
67. James 3:18 NLT
68. Matthew 6:15 NLT
69. Job 18:4 TEV
70. See Matthew 1:21
71. Romans 5:11 TLB
72. Acts 10:35 *The Message*
73. See Luke 15:7

PHOTO CREDITS

The
P. E. A. C. E.
Plan

The P.E.A.C.E. Plan is a worldwide grassroots strategy to attack the five greatest problems that affect billions of people: spiritual emptiness, corruption, poverty, disease, and illiteracy. P.E.A.C.E. stands for Promoting reconciliation, Equipping servant leaders, Assisting the poor, Caring for the sick, and Educating the next generation.

Launched by Rick Warren's Saddleback Church in 2003, over 8,000 volunteers working in small teams tested the plan in 68 countries. Today the PEACE Coalition includes churches, businesses, governments, and individuals partnering together around the world.

You can make a difference in the world as a PEACE Partner!

Email rick@thepeaceplan.com for information and visit www.thepeaceplan.com